Differentiated Leadership

Meeting Leaders where they are and getting them to where they need to be, yourself included.

Kiesha King-Brown

Copyright © 2018 KK Brown

All rights reserved.

ISBN: 9781731024756

DEDICATION

To my son, Jordan, for inspiring me strive to be the best possible version of me as an example for you, and inspiring me to provide you learnings from all aspects of my leadership journey.

To my husband, Columbus, for being my biggest career enthusiast.

CONTENTS

1	THE LEADERSHIP LENS	Pg. 1
2	THE COMMON WAYS LEADERS LEARN	Pg. 8
3	LEADER SELF-DEVELOPMENT AND PERSONAL BRAND	Pg. 13
4	LEADING LEADERS IN UNIQUE PLACES	Pg. 19
5	THE DNA OF LEADERSHIP	Pg. 30
6	WOMEN IN LEADERSHIP	Pg. 54
7	EFFECTIVE INTERVIEWING	Pg. 58
8	EFFECTIVE SELECTION	Pg. 63
9	TRAINING FOR AND MANAGING PERFORMANCE	Pg. 65
10	BUILDING A COHESIVE AND EFFECTIVE TEAM	Pg. 82
11	DECISION MAKING THAT MAKES SENSE	Pg. 86
12	GOAL SETTING AND STRATEGY	Pg. 90
13	ADOPTING AN ENTREPRENURIAL MINDSET	Pg. 93

1

THE LEADERSHIP LENS

Though often perceived simply as a state of entitlement, a position, an air of command, leadership is a process. If we stop for a moment to mentally step outside of the business environment we can view the process of leadership through the lens of everyday roles and activities. Take for instance gaining clarity around leadership through the lens of a fitness connoisseur. In this example, weight loss is the process. The weight loss is not something that is awarded based on effort exerted that day, or during a week, or based on achievements from the year prior. It is not granted because there is a strong desire to change bad habits or change behavior. It must be earned daily by putting in work beyond the levels of comfort. There must be commitment to the tedious part of the process.

When viewing leadership as a process, we must build

each isolated leadership muscle-building vision; inspiring, building a team, planning, prioritizing, assessing, analyzing, delegating, developing, creating a culture of accountability, etc. to build the leadership muscle as a whole. The company leading performance on last year's annual reporting, the fact that the important presentation was nailed in the prior month, and the awards applauding our leadership hanging above the desk are no more relevant to the existence of leadership today than the post graduate degree received documenting our educational expertise. Leadership is earned through daily behavior and daily interactions with others that add visible value and show increasing impact on behalf of the company.

With that said, the difference between good leadership and exceptional leadership can be dependent on the leader's ability to lead different personalities and different leadership styles in the way that enables and inspires them independent of others.

By definition, differentiate is "to make or become different in the process of growth or development." Differentiated leadership is leadership beyond the title and the company lanyard. The bridge between how you lead and how a person's mindset, behavior, execution and/or performance are influenced is the differentiator in your leadership. As a leader you can differentiate yourself from other leaders and with those you lead through the content you teach, the process you use, how you communicate, how you follow up, as well as the learning environment you create.

Differentiated leadership can be identified by a combination of characteristics and behavior. How others perceive your degree of honesty and transparency will be different than how those things may be perceived in other leaders. Do you seem sincere? Do your motives align with your message? Are you forthcoming or do you tend to hoard critical information for yourself? In addition to being honest and transparent, is your communication consistently clear? Do others understand your point of view? Can others count on you to make a complex message simple without feeling like you had to "dumb it down" for them? Are the takeaways from your communication different from the intention of your communication? Is your communication consistent in a manner that is timely, relevant and shared with urgency when applicable? The consistency can also impact the perception of transparency and clarity.

Do you possess a humble confidence? In the business environment, we often place leaders in one of two categories, humble or confident. Those that portray both significantly differentiate themselves from their peers. It takes mindful talent to be both. Humble confidence is assurance in your vision, strategy, and direction without the side effect of arrogance. It is confidence in your team expressed verbally and through action that involves recognition and the invitation to contribute without feeling threatened. It is confidence in the team's ability to assist in overcoming challenges and to rebound from failures versus bearing all the weight on your shoulders per the belief that only you can make it happen.

Do you assume positive intent? Do you have a

contagious optimism that gives you the ability to breathe life into a vision, an idea, a strategy, a thought process in a way that compels another to believe in it and/or respond to a call of action because of it? Do you point out silver linings to keep your team motivated when their efforts seem futile? Do you balance your conversation with encouragement in moments where you must communicate where others fell short or failed to execute?

Do you delegate the right projects to the right people to make the most progress? Do you delegate in a way that is mutually beneficial versus just to the benefit of you as a leader? Does the delegation of projects or tasks get additional things accomplished but also increase the other person's knowledge or skill set?

Is your leadership a reflection of intuitiveness? Do you lead with the ability to strongly perceive fact, the truth; to have insight around something in a way that proves true without process of tangible reason? Is your gut instinct always on point? Do your quick natured assumptions tend to prove effective relative to the goals and strategy?

Are you willingly and consistently collaborative partnering in a way that shows curiosity and respect for others input and points of view? Do you have the presence of being in charge without showing up as the boss? Can others sense an insatiable thirst for execution and excellence? Do you create a learning environment with the desire and the ability to unlock the potential in a leader's growth that others could not or that the leader did not see in him/herself?

The best leaders can gain leadership insight from almost any situation. Take martial arts, it exists on the principles of self-discipline, respect, courtesy, goal-setting, phases of progress and excellence. Martial arts teachers are also like leaders in the business world because they teach students of different ages, different genders, different backgrounds, different levels of experience and learning curves often at the same time. To be effective they must meet their students where they are just as leaders must meet the diverse group of team members where they are in order to develop them and to enable them to achieve their goals.

If you have met someone who is a Master Gardener, you would know that he must create a habitat that allows his vegetables or herbs to successfully grow. Similarly, leaders must create conditions for success for their team to grow through training development, providing the right tools and resources. Not only must leaders provide resources, like gardeners who must remove weeds, leaders must remove anything that threatens or impedes the growth of the team. This could be a toxic member of the team, conflicts within the team, lack of training, losing as a habit, lack of confidence, being understaffed or any other hindrances.

I've told every team I've had the pleasure of leading that boss is a four-letter word. My expectation is that they take ownership in their own leadership journey and the trajectory of their business. Leadership can be compared to driver's education. Like Driver's Education, they should be in the driver's seat with me as support when needed. I will always have the ability to brake on their behalf to avoid imminent danger; or take the wheel temporarily from my seat to get us headed back in the right direction. But the responsibility is on the "student" to consistently show they can drive their business in the right direction in spite of any roadblocks.

We've all had the misfortune of having a computer malfunction to the degree that we have had to call the help desk or partner with IT to get the computer functioning properly. The computer may even have had to get a virus removed. In many cases, the IT department has had to temporarily take control of the computer and reconfigure it, reset it, remove the virus so that it is able to function effectively again. Sometimes as a leader, whether in person or virtually, it is necessary to help someone on our team remove a virus or fixed mindset, to reset expectations and/or to reconfigure certain behaviors to get the team functioning effectively.

No offense to dogs or leaders, but leadership similarities can exist in dog training. To train a dog, supervision has to be provided and boundaries have to be set up front. Dogs also need to be taught and given a routine. They do better when expected behaviors feel like a habit.

Differentiated Leadership

Dogs respond much better to positive reinforcement for going to the bathroom outdoors versus in the house, for sitting when asked, for interacting with others as expected much better than they respond to punishment for not doing those things. In parallel, employees and other leaders are more effective and respond better to routines given, discipline that is outweighed by reward or acknowledgment and patience from their leader. Dog trainers also focus on agility training. This type of training teaches dogs to move effectively around, through or over the obstacles they will encounter. The trainer often starts by physically showing the dog how to do what is expected and then from there verbally coaches them through it. Leaders must teach agility relative to professional obstacles real or perceived and start with leading by example.

Not unlike students in a school environment, leaders and teams have diverse learning needs. They receive and process information in unique ways. Leaders find value in a boss or mentor who makes the time to teach them and is invested in their learning and growth. Experts have identified several common ways of learning. These include, but may not be limited to, auditory learners, visual learners, kinesthetic learners, logical learners.

2

THE COMMON WAYS LEADERS LEARN

Leaders don't necessarily hear, absorb and retain information in the same way. Therefore, they also learn in a way unique to their own personality and mindset. It is important that those who lead leaders and/or employees understand the different types of learning styles and use that knowledge to create a learning environment most engaging for others. There are four learning styles that should be considered: auditory, visual, kinesthetic, and logical.

> *Auditory learning* is a learning style in which a person learns through hearing and active listening. An auditory learner is dependent on hearing information as a main way of learning. They will typically retain around 75% of what they hear. Information not heard will have minimal relevance. They also use their

listening and repeating skills to sort through the information that is communicated. They are good at memorization, noticing sound effects, talking, and are often articulate communicators.

Characteristics of Auditory Learners:

- They talk about what to do, about the pros and cons of a situation. They indicate emotion through the tone, pitch, and volume of their voice.
- They physically try things out, touch, feel, and manipulate objects.
- They repeat facts often with their eyes closed.
- They will use word association to remember information.
- They will record information and listen to the recordings repeatedly.
- They will avoid any auditory distractions.

If you are an auditory learner, you make up 30% of the population.

Visual learning, also referred to as the Spatial learning style, is a style in which a learner utilizes graphs, charts, maps, pictures and diagrams. Visual learners remember 75% of what they see.

Characteristics of Visual Learners:

- Remember what they read rather than what they hear.

- Prefer reading a story rather than listening to it.

- Learn from seeing things written out on a whiteboard.

- Use diagrams and charts to understand ideas and concepts.

- Take notes during meetings, while listening to presentations or during a conversation.

- Study by looking over things.

- Love books and magazines.

- Often have impressive photographic memories.

- Tend to be detail oriented.

- Are often organized.

- Have trouble recalling someone's name but will remember their face.

If you are part of the 65% of the population that consider themselves visual learners, you are in good company with people like Albert Einstein and Steven Spielberg.

Kinesthetic learning or Tactile learning is a learning style in which learning takes place by the leaders carrying out physical activities, rather than listening to a facilitator or watching videos. This learning style involves touching and engaging with objects and material in order to learn.

Characteristics of Kinesthetic learners:

- Often feel the need to be moving and have trouble sitting still.

- Quickly learn based on what they are doing, and the learning is long term.

- May excel in physical activities such as martial arts, dance, sports, etc.

- Possess above average hand-eye coordination.

- When talking, their hands are moving as much as their lips.

- Enjoy exercising and often have epiphanies when active.

- Remember information better when they have written it down versus when they have typed it or read it.

- May stand up in a meeting instead of sitting down to improve comprehension and memory of the information.

If you are a kinesthetic learner, consider yourself unique. About 5% of the population learn tactically including David Copperfield and Michael Jordan.

Logical-mathematical learning style refers to the ability to reason, solve problems, and learn using numbers, abstract visual information, and analysis of cause and effect relationships. Logical-mathematical learners are typically methodical and think in logical or linear order.

Characteristics of Logical learners:

- Enjoy mental challenges.
- Easily see correlations or relationships between concepts.
- Use deductive reasoning.
- Gain energy from problem solving.
- Have an investigative nature.
- Naturally identify trends and patterns.
- Appreciate facts to back up opinion or theory.
- View problems as puzzles.

Do you relate to the logical learning style? You may have some things in common with Bill Gates, Albert Einstein and Sir Isaac Newton.

3

LEADER SELF-DEVELOPMENT AND PERSONAL BRAND

Before we can take the lead with other leaders most effectively, we must first understand our own learning styles and learn to lead ourselves. We are the most challenging leader we will ever have to manage. To be effective we must create our own routine of learning and understand our own learning style. We must be clear on our leadership deficiencies and what we need to do to impact them and have clarity around our strengths and how to best utilize them. This clarity will enable a leader to build a team around them that balances the leader and helps them with any competencies that don't lie within his/her strengths.

There are Five Phases of Leadership that each leader will go through as a part of his/her personal growth journey

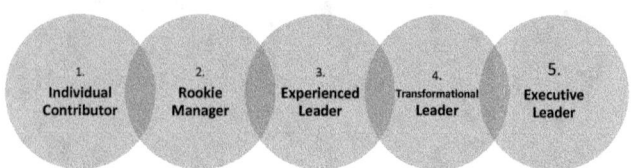

1. Individual Contributor-In this phase a person may have a leadership or manager title but does not have any direct reports. This is when the foundation of credibility and reputation of performance should be built. Developing a network should also be initiated in this early phase.

2. Rookie Manager-At this point a person will have at least 1 or 2 employees that report to him/her. His/her role will evolve in complexity and he/she will need to develop organizational and time management skills.

3. Experienced Manager/Leader-Phase 3 is where a leader has a substantial amount of leadership experience on his/her resume. He/she has mastered managing the team, managing time, and managing tasks. The growth of the leader will progress to one who has a global organizational lens and perspective.

The leader will also stabilize partnerships in his/her network at this point and master collaboration.

4. Transformational Leader-This is the phase where leaders can truly start to differentiate themselves. They will become increasingly strategic, be a subject matter expert at developing other leaders, exhibit emotional leadership skills and be accountable for more complex teams and critical results.

5. Executive Leader-This is the final phase of leadership yet it is one that is ever evolving. It is indicative of one who leads decision makers, influencers, thought leaders and those who function as pillars of the company's success and future. These leaders are often officers of the company or members of the C-Suite.

Part of a leader taking ownership for self-growth is learning from other leaders' successes but learning from personal missteps and failures. Finding a way to use failures as a means for self-reflection and learning, versus as a setback, allows for all parts of the journey to be a means for development and leadership maturation. Part of self-development also includes focusing on behaviors more than focusing on outcomes. Doing so helps a leader to both build and sustain personal growth but also start to teach a leader how to build culture outside of himself or herself.

As a leader experiences and exhibits growth, a personal brand will become associated with his/her leadership. It is important for all leaders to decide what their brand should reflect. It may reflect confidence, humility, competitiveness, people development, top tier performance, humor, strategic thought process, creativity, articulateness, community or other things that are important to who they are. The ability to influence and manage the impressions others have minimizes others' assumptions and keeps others from 'filling in the blanks' because there is uncertainty about a leader's brand.

Personal Branding is the ongoing process of establishing a positive and desirable impression based on the perception of others. Your personal brand is a representation of who you are, what you have accomplished, and the potential you have to accomplish or impact other things. It is how others perceive the hinge point between your communication, your behavior and your results. Simplified it is your own personal marketing strategy.

Take a moment to consider how your brand as a person and leader currently shows up.

Differentiated Leadership

What's Your Brand?

- How do others descibe you when you're not around?
- How would you describe yourself?
- What are the disconnects?
- How does what you wear/how you wear it impact your brand?
- How do you flex your influential muscles?
- How do you allow yourself to be infuenced?
- What precedents do you set for how others interact with you?
- How do you recognize or show appreciation for others?

If you're like most, there are probably some things you would like to change about your personal brand. Here are some steps to get you started:

- ➢ Build necessary skills. Find a vehicle for training and development.
- ➢ Find a credible mentor to champion you.
- ➢ Make it a habit of seeking personal feedback and allow changes made based on that feedback to be visible to others.
- ➢ Craft and own your elevator speech.
- ➢ Be consistent.
- ➢ Implement a plan to work on the behaviors that will change your brand as intended. Partner with a coach to build the plan.
- ➢ Intentionally interact with those you want to perceive you differently and engage with different behaviors.
- ➢ Show how you can add value to those you want to have a better perception of you.

> Contribute more on calls and in meetings with a positive and value-added perspective.
> Acknowledge when someone else shares a perspective that you find value-added.

Once you learn to lead and manage your own unique characteristics and manage your personal leadership brand, you will be well equipped to start preparing to lead others and meet them where they are. You will be able to effectively lead other leaders in their own individual and unique places.

4

LEADING LEADERS IN UNIQUE PLACES

Leaders who lack confidence

Leaders must lead as a reflection of their title.

I'm sure we've all seen the classic movie The Wizard of Oz. In that movie one of the key characters is the cowardly lion. This character is a notable oxymoron. He is the king of the forest, yet he lacks courage. His mindset and behavior are not reflective of his title.

Similarly, leaders often lack managerial courage which can be described as the ability and confidence to communicate direct and actionable feedback to leaders at all levels, in moments of conflict and in ways that add value. Managerial courage typically reflects bold, confident leadership. It embraces the courage to empower one's team to challenge or disagree with your thought process as a leader. A leader that does not possess managerial courage lacks the wholistic essence of leadership.

To gain managerial courage one must build and learn to flex several muscles. Some of these include:

- Take the initiative to be a change agent, to lead change positively, to help others understand the purpose and need for change. To bring others along on the journey.

- Be transparent and consistent about self-accountability.

- Be strong enough to recognize your mistakes and humble enough to let your team know you are aware of them, and that you are open to taking the team as a partner to minimize them.

- Be comfortable being uncomfortable. Be willing to be the one juror who says 'not guilty' in a room of intense pressure to conform. Practice being in the uncomfortable in an effort to draw confidence from uncertainty or risk.

- Step up and make the tough decisions in the heat of the moment.

- Have the courage to lead in the moment. Address issues, provide coaching, give constructive feedback in the moment without delay.

Ensure in every moment your mindset and behavior are reflective of your title and your potential to influence.

ADHD Leaders

Nearly 17 Million Americans are impacted by ADHD. Around 4.4% of Adults have been diagnosed with ADHD. ADHD, or Attention Deficit Hyperactivity Disorder, is a neurodevelopmental disorder. Characteristics of this disorder include an ongoing pattern of inattention, hyper focus on one task a person finds enjoyable, challenges with short term memory, impulsive activity, disorganization, chronic tardiness, consistent boredom. ADHD is highly genetic and is treatable. Those who seek treatment are enabled to function in the workplace significantly more effectively with the right medication vs. without medication.

With that said, a good percentage of adults with ADHD are extremely intelligent, creative and successful above the average. Sir Richard Branson of Virgin America, actor Will Smith, singer Justin Timberlake, singer Solange Knowles, Terry Bradshaw formerly of the Pittsburgh Steelers, journalist Lisa Ling, and Pulitzer prize winner Katherine Ellison are examples of very successful leaders/people that have publicly shared they have been diagnosed with ADHD.

In many cases, it may be hard to identify a leader with ADHD. For female leaders ADHD can be very different with different symptoms. Females develop symptoms later in life and are less hyperactive, less impulsive, more disorganized, more forgetful and tend to be more introverted. Females that go undiagnosed may come across as anxious or depressed.

Your ability to lead a leader with ADHD can aide in the success of that leader and his/her development. Key elements to be aware of to support an ADHD leader are:

- Time Management

    o The challenge of inattention creates opportunity in a leader's ability to manage their time. You can support by giving clear timelines for projects, doing more frequent check-ins to ensure the leader is staying on task, having the leader key reminders into their calendar or their phone for audible reminders to help them stay on track. ADHD leaders commonly miscalculate how long a task or project will take. Having a discussion with them prior to each project and gaining alignment will help minimize the disconnect between their perception and the expectation.

- Acknowledgement and Reward

    o Acknowledgement will help to channel the energy and direct the leader's focus to the priorities. This can be verbal confirmation of a job well done on a frequent basis or another type of reward provided by the company for milestones achieved on a longer-term assignment.

- Lack of acknowledgement at a minimum will easily discourage an ADHD leader from continuing his/her focus and energy relative to the expectations.

- Prioritization

  - For a leader with ADHD everything feels urgent. What are clear priorities to most may not have any variation of urgency in the mind of a leader with ADHD. You will need to slow down with the leader and have dialogue about each of the tasks that needs to be completed, due dates, what other processes or departments those tasks may impact, consequences of not getting each of them done. Based on that, help the leader self-discover the order in which he/she should focus on the tasks.

Rookie Leaders

Rookie leaders can be those taking on their first leadership role and transitioning from a team member to the head of a team. A rookie leader may also be a leader who has leadership experience but is in a new role that requires different skills, has different expectations or requires him/her to lead a different level of leader than they have led before.

It's important to create an environment and relationship with a new leader that encourages him/her to ask lots of questions, responds positively when he/she is vulnerable enough to admit he/she doesn't understand something in the training process, is consistent with checking in to make sure he/she is confident in his/her ability to apply what is being learned. Supporting the new leader also means giving permission to fail and learn. Equipping a new leader with the following tips will help to shorten the learning curve, help him/her to quickly get comfortable in the new shoes he/she has to fill and start getting others to follow his/her lead:

- Listen to learn. Take notes, share feedback, but make the focus of listening learning.

- Learn to grow. Ask lots of questions, solicit feedback, observe senior leaders, engage in training opportunities, hook up with a mentor, read leadership books, etc.

- Don't fall into the mindset of assumptive execution. Put checks and balances in place to ensure expectations are being met relative to behaviors and financials on a consistent basis.

- Never let your title encourage you to lead with a sense of entitlement.

- Put 80% of your efforts and energy into the 20% of things that are most critical and that will give you the biggest return.

- Be Teflon. Don't let feedback, criticism or a bad day stick to you. Learn from it and move on.

- Be your team's bullet proof vest. Shield your team from unnecessary negative vibes, criticism and morale drainers. Take the fall for team underperformance.

- Learn to wear both the coach and the cheerleader uniform at the same time. Never let a coaching moment go unaddressed but be your team's biggest fan and encourager. Both will increase your team's loyalty to you and the company.

- Have an allergic reaction to mediocrity. Don't be so connected to your teams' emotions that you validate them to the point where it becomes okay to just be good enough.

- Know that you've never arrived as a leader. Success is a moving target.

Cocky Leaders

Cocky leaders have all the answers and possess an inability to learn from others, sometimes even those they report to. They are not receptive to feedback and may be dismissive of others' point of view. They talk more than they listen. They don't come across as genuine. Cockiness causes a leader to care more about himself/herself and his/her own success than the team or other leaders. Cocky leaders will often sacrifice relationships, required processes, and/or integrity to improve personal status, performance or perception.

The first step in growing a cocky leader is giving direct, constructive feedback around the state of his/her leadership and giving him/her clarity that change is required. The leader needs to understand how this type of leadership impacts others and that it could potentially be a career staller.

Whether the perception of arrogance is being driven by intentional or unintentional behavior, give the leader a couple specific things to do to create a more approachable perception. Some examples include:

- Take the initiative to speak to/greet others in a friendly manner before they greet you.

- Ask 1 or more leaders or peers for feedback weekly and let others see you are putting aspects of the feedback into practice. This can be a recurring event scheduled on the calendar.

- Facilitate a feedback session with the team and have the team anonymously write down their thoughts. It can be in the form of "I like" and "I wish". This will let the leader know what the team likes about his/her leadership and wants the leader to continue doing. It will also shed light on what they would like to see differently. Gather the common themes and discuss with the leader and partner on an action plan based on the learnings.

High Potential Leaders

The top performing 25% of any leadership team are the high-potentials. These are the leaders who tend to carry the weight when it comes to the team or organization as a whole achieving its goals. These leaders often get taken for granted because of their consistency of contribution and may feel neglected as more focus tends to be placed on the under performers.

High potential leaders need the same amount of partnership but that partnership needs to be differentiated from those with other leaders. Top performing leaders need to be challenged. They need someone to inspire a personal vision that helps them to see how they can continue to maximize their potential.

A high potential leader I had the pleasure of working with ran her area of the business like a tight ship. The consistency of operational processes, training, follow up, execution of company direction, and financials was impressive. This leader's team respected her ability to be stern and her level of expectation. Every member on her team was loyal to her and took pride in contributing to the team's success.

Because of the excellence she brought as a leader daily she hadn't gotten any constructive criticism, which I like to call growth feedback. She also hadn't gotten any development. There was an assumption by her previous leaders that she was good to go. While I appreciated her performance and her consistency, I saw more in her. I saw untapped potential that could take her leadership to an even higher level. I saw opportunity that could be a career staller if she wanted to move to the next level. This leader had the epitome of effective communication with her team, but outside of her comfort zone her communication was less than articulate. She was redundant in her message which made it hard for others to understand her key point. She became very nervous and did not communicate in a manner which flowed so that others could follow her thought process.

I was able to help this leader be proactive and jot down the points she wanted to get across well in advance of a conversation or presentation and then practice relaying those points in a concise manner. I partnered with her on presentations to her peers with practice before, feedback in the moment, and hind-sighting after. I shared tips and tricks to help her read the audience and be able to adjust in the moment when presenting. That high potential leader was able to grow while still being acknowledged for being the best of the best as a leader overall.

Bottom Performing Leaders

Leaders who are not meeting goals and expectations are at a crossroads. They will need to have a discussion giving them clarity around the two paths they can take. One path involves them changing their behavior quickly and consistently to get back on track. The less fortunate path leads to demotion or termination. This is based on inability or the choice not to change behavior or continued underperformance.

It is often beneficial to revisit the job description with the leader. Have him/her highlight the things he/she is doing consistently in one color and highlight what he/she does inconsistently in another color. Anything that is not being executed at all can remain un-highlighted. Doing this takes the emotional bias out of the self-assessment of his/her execution.

An action plan for the leader should be written in partnership with him/her. The plan should include 1-3 behavioral competencies or things identified in the job description that the leader needs to focus on, what behaviors need to be observed relative to those competencies, how the improvement will be measured tangibly, and how often they will check in and with whom. A minimum of weekly check-ins will give the best indication of the leader's ability to adjust and execute as discussed.

5

THE DNA OF LEADERSHIP

While leaders learn and lead in their own way, there are some characteristics that will make every leader more effective and give them more credibility.

Confident Leadership

Confidence can make or break the leader with the most experience, the most education, the most skill and the most value to add. Confidence impacts command presence. We all know that leader or person who walks into a room and you know they walked in without even turning around. They walk with intention. Even if they don't speak a lot, when they do speak people pay attention. They are articulate and speak with clarity. They speak in a way that is engaging. On a break at a meeting, it is likely that others are flocking to interact with them vs. the other way around. Their reputation may precede them.

Confidence also impacts credibility and perception of trustworthiness. If someone appears to lack confidence others may not be confident that what the leader is communicating is factual or believable. The degree of confidence perceived also impacts the degree of engagement from a team or audience. The leader must have control of both the content being communicated and the room or stage. He/she has to have perception of power whether he/she is formally or informally in charge.

"A good leader inspires others with confidence in him. A great leader inspires them with confidence in themselves." -Unknown

Lack of confidence is the kryptonite to leadership no matter the talent, skill or potential. There are very few leaders who have 100% confidence 100% of the time. The key is being able to project confidence in spite of your nervousness and constantly evolving your comfort zone. Here are some thoughts to help you build confidence in a leader.

- Meetings: Before going to a meeting or conference have the leader plan out his presence. If it's a 3-day meeting have him decide how many times each day he will raise his hand to grab the mic runner's attention or to share his thoughts with the group. Will he speak once before lunch and once after? If you have the agenda in advance-which topics would he be comfortable speaking about? He should be prepared with thoughts on those specific topics. This will give him confidence because he is prepared. It will also minimize someone calling on him to speak about something when he doesn't have value to add.

- Conference Calls: If he is the facilitator, have him plan the agenda and his speaking points well in advance. Have him anticipate questions and be prepared with potential answers. Have him ask a few participants in advance if they will chime in when he opens the call up for discussion so there is no awkward silence.

- Interviews: As the participant, make sure he does his homework. He must become the subject matter expert on the company he is interviewing with, their values, their culture, their competition, their industry. He should make sure he is the subject matter expert on his own resume. Some interviewers will go point by point on a resume and deep dive into the information. Ensure he is prepared to articulately speak to examples to back up what he has written and how he can add value to their organization based on his experience.

- Presentations: Have the leader practice, practice and practice some more. The more he practices, the more comfortable he will be with the material, where key info is on the slides, anticipate questions, remain organized and on time. Practicing and being comfortable will also allow him to be himself and allow his personality to connect with the audience vs. being so focused on what his content is. Have him start with "baby steps". Have him co-facilitate a few trainings before leading one on his own. Have him do the icebreaker at a meeting prior to having him speak on a topic at a meeting. Gradually evolve his comfort zone.

- <u>Leading a New Team</u>: Confidence in leading your team starts and ends with genuine connection. The leader will need to get to know his team as individuals first before getting to know them as leaders. This is one of those situations where he will have to slow down to speed up. He should spend time with each of them one-on-one. He should get to know them and be vulnerable enough to allow them to get to know him as a person first. Once he's done that, encourage him to enjoy a team building with them as a group to strengthen the connection. The next step is to get to know them individually as leaders. What are their strengths and opportunities? What are their aspirations? How do they like to be led? What type of recognition do they appreciate? What motivates them? What's their perception of accountability?

Be sure to give your leader positive reinforcement when you see the leader's confidence in action. Enlist other key leaders to acknowledge improvement when they observe it as well. Don't forget to keep that balanced with direct and constructive feedback on where they still need to make progress. Your ability to be transparent around the opportunities observed and provide timely coaching will be even more valuable than the encouragement you are able to give.

"You gain strength, courage, and confidence by every experience in which you really stop to look fear in the face. You are able to say to yourself, 'I have lived through this horror. I can take the next thing that comes along.'" -Eleanor Roosevelt

"The most beautiful thing you can wear is confidence." - Blake Lively

"Show and Tell" Leadership

"Show and Tell" Leadership is a way to guide execution more effectively. If you use the example of follow up, having a leader physically show you the things they accomplished on their to-do list is a much more effective way to validate versus them just communicating completion. Again, sometimes we need to slow down and have tangible follow up versus assumptive follow up. Leaders will also be more detailed and thorough in their work if they know they will have to show you exactly what they accomplished.

Balanced Leadership

Balanced leadership is important to ensure consistent engagement of your team. This type of leadership is yet another example of where leaders need to slow down to speed up. They must slow down enough to observe behaviors worthy of recognition. The more a leader slows down to acknowledge what he/she sees being executed well, the more valued an employee will feel, the more incremental value he/she will continue to add to the customer experience, to other employees' experience, and to the financial gain of the company.

Recognition is one of the most powerful communication tools a leader has. The most impactful recognition is when it is unexpected: either based on what they are being recognized for, the timing of the recognition, and/or who the recognition is coming from, above and beyond an immediate boss. Employees appreciate and desire accountability as long as it is fair, consistent and balanced with notable recognition as applicable. The most ineffective and detrimental accountability is when it is unexpected and inconsistent.

With that in mind, balanced leadership requires that there is a balance of both recognition or acknowledgement and effective accountability. It requires more than just ensuring each exists. If the bar of accountability is raised at any point, the level of recognition must also blatantly increase. If recognition remains at the same level the team will have a perception that they simply live in an environment of accountability. Employees will always be more likely to recall negative influence than positive influence. This influence can evoke either negative or positive emotions in employees and are likely to be reflected in their demeanor or behavior. Unbalanced, the execution and influence of recognition and accountability can cause unnecessary frustration, lack of buy in and minimized engagement.

Adaptable Leadership

"You can't adjust the wind, but you can adjust the sails." - Elizabeth Edwards

For a moment, picture the captain of a boat potentially stuck in the middle of rough waters. She is focused on the wind and the challenges it is causing in her efforts to make forward progress towards her destination. She must change her focus from the wind to her own sails-that which she has control over, that which determines the "how".

Now, picture a leader who has become overwhelmed and caught up in the day-to-day challenges and frustrations in her work life. Picture a leader who is missing deadlines, late to calls, has inconsistent results, is feeling stagnant in her development, is struggling with the change of re-structure, has a new team she hasn't figured out how to lead, and/or is in a constant state of frustration. All of these things may represent the wind in her own personal state of 'rough waters'. As the captain her impact can be witnessed relative to how she guides the sails. As a leader, the adjustment of her 'sails' is simply the adjustment in how she is currently leading, how she guides her team, how she focuses on having a growth mindset vs a fixed mindset.

As a leader we will face winds of varying strengths. We must choose to rise up and lead in spite of the turbulence. We can adjust our 'sails' in numerous ways.

- Increase the amount of teaching/coaching with the team to improve their confidence and execution.

- Adopt a more questions-based approach. Seek to understand the employee or leader's mindset, frustrations and capabilities so that you can help the leader lead through what's getting in his/her way. That will allow you to also lead and execute more effectively.

- Seek additional employee and/or customer feedback to help you identify detours relative to your roadblocks.

- Implement reverse accountability. Let your team know when they are to follow up with you on their progress and execution. Have them take the initiative.

- Partner with a peer or mentor to help you see from an unbiased perspective with the blinders off. You will be able to proceed more objectively and engage in a leadership pivot that minimizes the impact of the 'wind' on your leadership.

Whether the captain or the leader, the goal remains the same. As a leader, you must always be aware of the "what" and be willing and able to adjust the "how" with urgency and thoughtfulness, so the goal is achieved in the expected timeframe. You must be willing to lead in the moment. You must be willing to revise your plan as needed and take partners as applicable. You must be willing to lead at the same level of effectiveness in the storm as you do when waters are still.

Organized Leadership

An Organized leader is a more effective and more consistent leader. There are seven responsibilities a leader can organize to make sure they are maximizing productivity and remain consistent in expectations.

1. PLANNING
    a. Long-Term-By Quarter, By Year, 3-Year, 5-Year. This is your strategic plan to get you from where you are in leadership, in processes and operations, and in results, to where you need to be. It should be aligned with both the vision and the mission.
    b. Monthly-Align what you need to accomplish for the month with company monthly expectations, monthly financial goals, a monthly project or project phase for a client.
    c. Weekly-Determine what needs to be done for the week and break it down by day.
    d. Daily-Make any adjustments to the day by day in the weekly plan based on additional information or commitments (an added conference call, a re-scheduled appointment, a client call that needs to be returned). Schedule anything that is re-occurring daily.

2. TASKING
    a. **Priority**-Impact on boss, team, shareholders, clients, etc. Lack of execution will create a negative domino

Differentiated Leadership

> effect for other key pieces of the business.
>
> b. **Urgent**-Time bound but does not produce a domino effect and does not necessarily impact others.
> c. **Necessary**-Must be completed. Deadline is flexible. There is no impact to others. Minimal risk relative to execution.

3. ASSESSMENT AND ANALYSIS
   a. Block out a specific day or time of each day (for example 8am-9:30am Monday-Thursday) for any needed assessment or financial analysis for consistency.
   b. Schedule time on your calendar for when you need to communicate the analysis and supporting information.
   c. Set up your reports to autogenerate on a certain day.

4. NOTETAKING
   a. Keep a separate notebook for meeting notes, one for conference call notes, one for miscellaneous in the moment items. Or label them by time period. When you need to locate a specific portion of notes you will know where to find them.
   b. Minimize notes taken on sticky notes, index cards, napkins, etc. These are easy to lose and hard to find when needed.

5. COMMUNICATION
   a. Phone Calls-Return as soon as possible for important calls. 1-3 hours.
   b. Emails-Return emails within 24 hours. If you don't have the information requested

send an email that lets them know you received the email and will respond once you have the information.
   c. Chat/Text-Respond within 10-20 minutes at least to acknowledge receipt.

6. **FOLLOW UP**
   a. Follow up on execution-Follow up on direction given by you or the company. Calendar tap yourself and notate the follow up as an event reminder.
   b. Follow up on the follow up-Follow up to ensure that your leader is validating execution. Calendar tap yourself and notate the follow up as an event reminder. You can also calendar tap the leader so they know when you will be following up.
   c. Reverse follow up-Give your leader direction to follow up with you to validate his/her execution. Give him/her a deadline and let him/her know to initiate the follow up.

7. **WHITESPACE**
   a. Schedule at least 2-4 hours per week for literally nothing. This will give you flexibility for any unforeseen tasks that may arise.
   b. Dedicated space on your calendar will also allow you time for purposeful and uninterrupted time for planning.

Change Management Leadership

"Success in management requires learning as fast as the world is changing." -Warren Bennis

If you've ever used a travel agent, you know his/her role is to sell, arrange and provide guidance as he/she engages with clients. Depending on the client they may travel by train, airplane, car, bus, etc. Each client may need a different means of travel even if he/she is headed to the same destination. The travel agent also focuses on making sure the client will be comfortable once the client arrives at their destination. That could mean finding a hotel that suits personality and needs, restaurants suited to his/her tastes, specialists to help once he/she arrives.

While being a travel agent is probably much more adventurous, leaders will have to function as change agents in a very similar fashion multiple times throughout their career. When you find yourself in the role of change agent it is your priority to 'sell' your team and/or other leaders on the vision relative to the change the company is going through. The change requires employees to engage in a journey relative to the direction the company will now take. Change without buy-in leads to conflict between the expectation and the execution. It hinders collaboration and stalls growth.

Once you've helped others understand and gain buy-in around the change it will be necessary to provide guidance relative to their role in the change and how they too can bring others along. Every member of your team will be adapting to the same company change. But, just as you lead differently with each individual, you will also need to meet them where they are in adapting to the change and provide their own personal vehicle to their new definition of success. Your continued presence, support and leadership in addition to providing them with other needed resources will help redefine their comfort zone for them.

Being a change agent means more than communicating the change. It's being accountable for the change in a way that enables and empowers others to embrace and lead through the change as well.

Empathetic Leadership

"When you start to develop your powers of empathy and imagination, the whole world opens up to you." –Susan Sarandon.

Empathetic Leadership is really about being aware, present and understanding as a leader. It is about implementing a daily practice of pausing for people. Those we lead need to feel they and their work are valued. Being empathetic is not about transfer or diminishment of power but more about finding a way to bridge leadership and genuine partnership. It's taking the time to look from the other person's "lens" versus simply from your own perspective. It's about leading by example with others that you want to care about your vision and that of the organization.

An empathetic approach to leadership allows for the balance between any narcissistic tendencies and true leadership. There are two simple, yet tedious things you can do to be a more empathetic leader.

1. Focus. Start focusing on being an attentive listener in all environments and relative to all communication vehicles.
2. Encourage. Encourage others to share their perspectives. This will allow you to identify root causes and impacts of behavior.

Communicative Leadership

"The art of communication is the language of leadership."
-James Humes

Communication is a vital component of effective relationships, effective teamwork and effective leadership. *Vital* in the description is crucial, imperative, essential, necessary. Without effective communication a leader becomes independent in his/her efforts with the inability to connect to others. Lack of effective communication prohibits the leader from being able to connect others to and inspire others towards the vision. It allows for disengagement and misses in execution.

Leaders by nature of authority given are always perceived

as communicating. Every look, every facial expression, every hand gesture, every word communicates to those around them. My entire leadership career I have been guilty of excessive facial expressions. It's hereditary and something that at times I have no control over. Based on both feedback and reaction over the years, I've learned to ensure that others are aware of my talent of facial expressions and are comfortable asking me what I'm thinking so there is no miscommunication.

Some leaders have to be very cognizant of their hand gestures. Unintentionally, lack of hand gestures could give the perception that a leader is not passionate or bought in to what he/she is communicating. Conversely, a leader with an exaggerated amount of hand gestures could come across as aggressive or nervous.

To improve effectiveness of communication a leader can either be aware of or improve upon the following points:

- <u>Understand the audience in advance</u>. Whether it is one person, or a group of people understand what's important to them, understand if they prefer quick facts or thorough details, understand if they are engaged by storytelling.

    Understand how to connect the dots between what you are communicating and the role they are in. Understand attention spans-usually the higher the level of the leader the less lenience and attention they will give you.

- <u>Make sure communication is mutual</u>. Make a genuine effort to listen to enable additional engagement when you are talking or presenting.

- <u>Be transparent in communication</u>. When leaders don't keep others in the loop they start to make assumptions and fill in the blanks with information that isn't necessarily accurate. Leaders need to feel like they are a part of what's important.

- <u>Provide consistency of communication.</u> Others should be able to depend on and anticipate when they will receive communication. Pertinent information and response to emails/voicemails should be communicated in a timely and routine manner.

"TADA" Leadership

"Discipline is the bridge between goals and accomplishment." -Jim Rohn

Whenever my four-year old does something he deems impressive or something he's never accomplished before he excitedly shouts "tada" for all to hear. The term "tada" references a way to call attention to something, an exclamation of triumph or completion of something unexpected. "Tada" leadership metaphorically defines leadership that is worthy of drawing attention or portrays something exceptional that has been achieved. At its best, "Tada" leadership is triumph of exceeding expectations.

When considering expectations, most leaders consider the goal the finish line. However, driven leaders and the most successful perceive the goals as the minimum expectation. They see the expectations given as the starting line versus the finish line. This mindset takes focus and discipline.

To lead as a reflection of that discipline leaders can goal themselves 5%, 10%, 20% above what the company expectations are and build their strategy around the adjusted goal. Leaders can make an effort to do more than what is asked. For instance, if the expectation is to create a strategy, the leader can build and submit both the requested strategy as well as a contingency plan. If asked to facilitate a training the leader could reach out to the participants in advance and ask what would make the training most value added to them and then adjust the training to meet the participants where they are in their leadership journey.

Moral of the story is, leaders should always seek to execute with a wow factor. At the same time, the leader should keep balance with humility. It's important to show exceptional leadership coupled with exceptional humility. The value to the company based on the additional efforts should stand out far more than any additional value to the leader.

Strategic Leadership

"Strategy without tactics is the slowest route to victory. Tactics without strategy is the noise before defeat." -Sun Tzu

Perhaps one the most critical aspects of effective leadership is strategic leadership. Strategic leadership involves the ability to understand, envision, create and communicate a plan that connects the dots between where the company is and where it has goaled itself to be in the future. It is the ability of a leader to mentally absorb the complexities of the organization and simplify them into prioritized, actionable steps of execution. It is the most intelligent use of power. It is risk taking balanced with self-control. It is the ability to make the complex seem simple without dumbing it down. It is the ability to have a unique yet effective use of resources. It is possessing the gift that allows a leader to challenge, push back, and manage up without detriment to morale, partnerships, or business. It's the knack of distributing responsibility in a way that maximizes the potential of the full team.

Leaders that possess a strategic mindset lead in a way that enables transformation. They combine a sense of courage and complexity of thought process to make risky decisions. They involve employees and loyal customers in the creation of or revision of procedures, processes and services. It is second nature to strategic leaders to find ways to streamline processes and unlock the max potential in productivity. Strategic leaders know when to course correct and do it with urgency. They are visibly disciplined and portray mental endurance. They have the ability to positively impact the financial trajectory of the company.

Strategic leaders stay in tune with the company's strengths and weaknesses, the financial drivers and drainers, the vulnerabilities within the talent structure, any inefficiencies in the operational processes, the potential risk created by outdated technology, the threats of current or future competition. They use this info to create long term vision of where the company will need to be, how it needs to get there, and the talent needed to make it happen. They stay focused on proactively leading the company into the future without sacrificing needed experiences and performance in the present. They get buy in from other leaders about what's to come and their role in bringing it to fruition.

Strengths Based Leadership

"Master your strengths. Outsource your weakness." - Ryan Kahn

We've all heard of strengths-based leadership- competency focus to acknowledge and alleviate perception of opportunities. It's the investment in a leader's strengths to maximize potential vs. making efforts to minimize or eliminate weaknesses. It can also be the practice of leveraging the strengths of a team to maximize team collaboration, execution, and performance. Considering the strengths of a potential new leader and how the leader will add balance to an existing team is an effective way to enhance a strengths-based leadership team.

Truly understanding a leader's strengths can help to identify your own or another leader's greatest potential and their capacity as a leader. It can allow a leader to go from a good leader or even a top performer to the leader that sets the bar of expectation for a particular role in a company. There are several ways to identify leadership strengths. One of the most well-known is the *Gallup Strengths Finder*. This assessment designates each of the 34 themes to one of four domains. These domains include Strategic Thinking, Influencing, Executing and Relationship Building. The domains describe how leaders use their talents.

According to *gallupstrengthscenter.com* people who know and play to their strengths are six times more likely to be engaged at work. They are three times as likely to have an excellent quality of life, six times as likely to do what they do best every day, and 7.8% more productive in their role. Understanding and leading through one's unique prioritization of strengths helps a leader to lead at their very best.

The *Myers-Briggs Types Indicator* is a self-reflective questionnaire that gives leaders insight to how they perceive the world and their thought process around making decisions.

The traits of *Myers-Briggs* are:

- (E) Extroversion, (I) Introversion
- (S) Sensing, (N) Intuition
- (T) Thinking, (F) Feeling
- (J) Judging, (P) Perception

Extroversion is most often characterized by a tendency towards sociability, assertiveness, high energy and a comfort level with being the center of attention. Introversion on the other hand usually describes a person who focuses more on their own internal thoughts and feelings as opposed to looking for external or social stimulation. A person considered to be an introvert re-energizes by spending time alone vs. by spending time with others.

Sensing and Intuition are considered the two perceiving functions. They are used to gather information and help to understand how any new information is interpreted. Thinking and feeling are noted as the two judging functions and are used for rational decision making.

Differentiated Leadership

There are sixteen different personality types based on the survey. There is no aspirational personality type. They are all equal and the intent is to understand differences and how to relate with those differences as well as any commonalities.

DISC is a behavioral model that can also help leaders understand their strengths and behavioral tendencies. It stands for Dominant, Inspiring, Supportive, Cautious. A leader can have one or any combination of these traits. The *DISC* assessment not only provides self-awareness as a leader but also enlightens leaders on how they can improve their ability to make hiring decisions, train and develop leaders, communicate with other leaders, etc. It gives transparency to what motivates a person, what their fears are, how they like to be interacted with.

Dimensions of Personality:

	DOMINANT
SEEKS:	Control
STRENGTHS:	Administration Leadership Determination
DISLIKES:	Inefficiency Indecisions
DECISIONS:	Decisive

INFLUENCING	
SEEKS:	Recognition
STRENGTHS:	Persuading Enthusiasm Entertaining
DISLIKES:	Routines Complexity
DECISIONS:	Spontaneous

STEADY	
SEEKS:	Acceptance
STRENGTHS:	Listening Teamwork Follow-Through
DISLIKES:	Insensitivity Impatience
DECISIONS:	Conferring

COMPLIANT	
SEEKS:	Accuracy
STRENGTHS:	Planning Systems Orchestration
DISLIKES:	Disorganization Impropriety
DECISIONS:	Methodical

6

WOMEN IN LEADERSHIP

"In the future, there will be no female leaders. There will only be leaders." -Sheryl Sandberg

If I asked you to name several great leaders, what are the first few names that would come to mind? It's a conditioned response that we think of male leaders when asked about those who are great.

Jeff Bezos. Howard Schultz. Sir Richard Branson. Bill Gates.

I'm sure we've all heard of these leaders who are considered the definition of great and what they do is common knowledge. They have proven success and credibility. They've earned their pinstripes.

Sandra Day O'Connor, Former Supreme Court

Justice. Sheryl Sandberg, COO, Facebook. Mary Barra, CEO, General Motors. Maxine Waters, U.S. Representative. Michele Buck, CEO, Hershey's.

Maybe reading the names of these leaders who are both fierce and female is a reminder of names you are familiar with, or perhaps some of them you've never heard of. You see, male leadership has been entitled to a seat and a voice at the table. Meanwhile, despite education, experience, skill, capability the best of the best female leaders have had to earn their voice in the same forums. They have to earn a voice that is perceived as confident being careful not to be cocky. A voice that challenges status quo while being careful not to come across as a know it all or disrespectful. A voice that is direct without being seemingly abrasive. A voice that is listened to and received vs. just being part of the background noise.

Female leaders seek respect more than they seek reward

Females seek success beyond survival. They are driven by proving the naysayers wrong but in a way that does not compromise their values or their purpose. Female leaders are very conscientious of ensuring that they help to show the next generation what's possible. They become focused on being an example that unlike the lyrics of the song "It's a Man's Man's Man's World" by James Brown, it's a world any of us desire it to be, if we are determined enough to make it so.

The Importance of Mentorship

The role of mentorship for females can be a game changer. That's not to say that a female has to have a female mentor. A female leader may simply need a mentor willing to take notice of her strengths and provide her with purposeful feedback and development. This would also allow companies to identify those female leaders with true potential and engage them differently in preparation for succession or newly designed roles.

Confidence as a Competence not a Competition

Women must never allow fear, uncertainty or lack of confidence to influence them to engage in professional battle with other females. Women don't need anyone but themselves to give them permission to lead and lead from the helm. Women don't need to 'cut the line' of female leaders in order to have presence or success. When women see each other as just leaders so will others see them that way.

"You're not in competition with other women. You're in competition with everyone." -Tina Fey

As females, women often feel enormous pressure to fit in like 'one of the boys', to hang out and drink as they drink, to speak as they speak, to find humor as they find humor. Women must find pride in their individuality as they've created it and help others see the value in their differentiated presence.

Women feel pressure not to fail, not to make mistakes. This pressure comes from the unspoken (and sometimes spoken) feedback that women must be better to be viewed just as effective as male leaders. Women must wear their wedge heels, their stilettos, their ankle boots, their sandals with confidence, in every step identifying who they are and what they bring to the table. They must embrace failure as opportunity to learn and show other leaders how it's done.

"My best successes come on the heels of failures." - Barbara Corcoran

7

EFFECTIVE INTERVIEWING

In my leadership journey I have participated in numerous interviews and from both sides of the desk. As an interviewee my least impactful interviews were those that felt like I was being interrogated. The most frustrating interviews were those where I felt I was "guilty until proven innocent"- guilty of not being the qualified candidate the interviewer was looking for until I could prove otherwise as I stumbled through the verbal questions-based obstacle course. These types of interviews are very transactional and make it challenging to assess the true personality and leadership style of the hiring manager and the environment of the company. Transactional or traditional interviews can feel very systematic and in themselves lack personality.

I recall an interview where I sat in a chair in the middle of the room. Around me in a partial square formation were several desks and chairs where the interviewing panel assumed their positions. I've also participated in interviews where the hiring manager sat across from me braced in an intense stare while other leaders asked all the questions. I've longed for the moment I was able to get back to my car in interviews where every answer I gave was challenged in a scrutinized manner. In situations like these, the interview candidate never even gets the chance to really get to know the leaders and the interviewers never get to know the candidate below the surface. If offered the job, there will have been a missed opportunity to initiate a relationship and create a welcome environment that could easily be built on as the new employee assimilates.

As leaders we learn from both the bad and good situations. We learn what we don't want to mimic and we learn what we may want to add to our leadership arsenal. My best interview experiences have influenced the type of experience I create for candidates interviewing with me. While every experience is different based on the role, location and current needs, at the very core of every experience is the connection I encourage the candidate to make with me and anyone interviewing with me. I make sure I bring my full self to the interview. I show up with the humor, the pride of being a mother, the passion I have for the things I do outside of work and, the humility that has come from my learnings as a leader as well as transparency around how I have achieved success. I have often had the recruiter or the candidate reach out and tell me, the reason they decided be a part of the company started with the connection they felt with me and/or the team of interviewers with whom I collaborated. A mutual connection, in addition to the presence of desired leadership characteristics, is what results in an invitation to the team.

Having clarity around what value you want the potential new employee to add allows you to assess for the necessary qualities vs. rating candidates against a checklist or assessing them based on 'what we've always done.' Below are several of the top characteristics that have promise of effective leadership in today's environment.

- **Potential**-What does their experience and their intellectual horsepower tell you about their ability to do more than the job description in the future or to be promoted and add additional value?

- **Integrity**-Do they and will they stand firm in their personal values as well as the values of the company? Will they do the right thing even when it's the hardest thing to do?

- **Initiative**-Are they self-driven? Are they hungry? Do they execute before being given direction?

- **Drive**-Are they fueled by challenges and the need to exceed goals and expectations?

- **Connection** -Do you "click" with the candidate? Do you feel you can relate to the candidate? Is it

Differentiated Leadership

mutual? Do they seem to have a connection to the company and its values and vision?

- **Tech savvy**-Technology is of growing importance to every organization. Are they comfortable with technology? Is technology a part of their daily life? Do they understand its connection to your business?

- **Communication**-Are they articulate? Do they sound rehearsed or do they sound passionate and thoughtful? Will they be able to effectively communicate at all levels? What primary form of communication do they prefer? Does that align with how you communicate/the company communicates?

- **Collaboration**-Do they have examples of how they take partners on behalf of the greater good? Do they prefer to work independently or seem to think they have all the answers?

- **Learning and Feedback Agility**-What's their routine for learning? What are their learning sources? How do they apply the learnings? How often do they solicit personal feedback? Can they share instances when they have implemented feedback from different sources? How do they use feedback to grow even when it's tough to receive?

- **Ability to Lead**-How well do they meet leaders where they are vs. leading just the full team? Do they wear their title as a badge, or do they lead as a partner to the team? Do they bring others along? Do others choose to follow them based on their leadership style, vision, communication and ability to grow them?

Depending on the role, some roles may require validation beyond assessment. A portion of effective interviews can be hands on or realistic. In sales, a common skill validation technique may be to have the candidate sell you your product as if you were a top customer. In HR you may have the candidate role play how they would have a tough conversation with an employee. For a financial role, the candidate could be asked to give an assessment of the company based on a P&L statement and have to speak to how they would have a positive impact on the company based on that assessment. It's important to make all aspects of the interview process a priority and take the time to ensure there will be a return on investment from the talent you choose to infuse into the organization.

Keep in mind the interview is potentially the first step in a candidate's career journey. It sets the tone for future engagement and loyalty. Equally as notable, the interview is your opportunity to market your company's culture and brand, to get buy-in on your leadership, to set the tone and desire for a future long-term partnership. Make sure your process of interviewing starts prior to the candidates being scheduled. Get clear on the attributes you want and need in a leader and how you will assess them throughout the dialogue and interaction. Get clear on why a candidate should want to work for you and the company and how you will ensure that resonates in the interview. Get clear, get prepared, get engaged in a way that creates conditions for engagement for all involved and will allow for more than a transactional experience.

8

EFFECTIVE SELECTION

The quality and effectiveness of the selection process will dictate the success of the talent management process as a whole. Selection of the most qualified candidate will make the training process less tedious. The right candidate will be more receptive, will have higher learning agility, will be more engaged around the information, and will have a shorter learning curve when it comes to figuring out how to apply what they have learned. The right candidate will require less, if any, repetitive communication of what they are being taught and required to do.

If the right talent is hired, there will be fewer situations where performance management is required. They will make less mistakes and will learn from the mistakes they do make. They will rebound quickly from feedback and even seek it out consistently to ensure they are meeting expectations. If the candidate hired does not turn out to be a good fit, he/she will require additional time from his/her manager. He/she will need consistent formal coaching conversations and follow up and additional informal re-direction coaching in the moment. An ineffective team member also adds a burden to his/her peers by creating incremental work for them to complete. Any aspect of the job the leader is inefficient at or doesn't get completed will still have to be done and that usually causes a peer to pick up the slack. This will not only cause productivity issues but could also create issues in the morale of that person and morale issues for the team as a whole. Performance management is a necessary part of the talent process but can be minimized with an effective investment in the right talent to begin with.

Hi-potential talent is the most rewarding to partner with around development. These individuals usually have capacity above and beyond the role they were hired to do. They are usually self-driven and have a strong desire to outperform themselves on a regular basis. They don't wait for someone else to bring them along on their own development journey. The partnership between the right talent and the manager happens naturally and doesn't feel tedious. It allows the manager to empower the individual to take on additional assignments, to make decisions outside of the scope of his/her normal role. It allows the manager to creatively inspire him/her to take risks. It makes it much easier for the manager to provide conditions for success in that individual's current role and also for the foundation that will be a catalyst for them in transition to the next level.

9

TRAINING FOR AND MANAGING PERFORMANCE

Not to be confused with development, training is teaching or showing someone how to do the technical pieces of a job. Examples could be teaching a leader how to use accounting software, how to read a financial report, how to use the company tools and resources, where to find client information, when to partner with Human Resources, etc. As previously mentioned, people learn differently. If you refer to the learning style, either communicated by the leader or that you were able to identify, you will be able to build a training plan that caters to that individual's learning style and sets him/her up for success. A good leader will make the time to check in and make sure that the person being trained is feeling comfortable that he/she is in a learning environment that is most effective for him/her and seek to understand if there is anything they would like to spend more time on.

Training can be experienced in several different ways. It is common and usually most effective to use a combination of training vehicles to keep trainees engaged.

- Classroom facilitated training
    - The effectiveness in a classroom environment is dictated by the preparation, subject matter expertise, presence and ability to engage of the facilitator.
    - Classroom training allows for consistency of messaging and information to the participants.
    - A downside to classroom training may be that is does not cater to a specific individual's learning style or the state of knowledge they already have.
- Learning environment-Hands on training
    - Hands on training allows for realistic experience in what the employee will be expected to do once the training period ends.
    - This type of learning environment allows the trainee to ask questions that he/she may not necessarily know to ask if he/she weren't physically attempting to perform the functions.
    - This type of training serves as practice allowing the employee to be more confident and effective once he/she steps into the role.

- Web or mobile based training
    - This type of training involves instruction communicated over the internet or via a mobile based application.
    - It is a benefit to be able to allow an employee to train anywhere.
    - With millennial based employee teams increasing, mobile training can result in a better level of engagement.

- Video based training
    - Video training provides the convenience of being able to be done at an office, at home or anywhere else.
    - Typically, a video training will allow you to go at your own pace and will allow you to pick up where you left off.
    - This type of training is best for product education, basic onboarding, policy and procedure communication.

- Shadowing and observation training
    - In this type of training, the new employee will follow a tenured and effective employee around to see what the role looks like from day to day. The intent is for the new employee to see what good looks like in addition to seeing what the tasks will be.
    - The trainee can ask questions and in some cases transition into hands on training.

The training that newly hired talent receives can impact both engagement and retention in either a very positive way that results in ROI long-term or in a way that completely misses the mark and causes talent to regret the acceptance of the job offer. Great training includes:

- Partnership between the employee and the leader/HR. The hiring manager in partnership with Human Resources should start with taking the time to understand what strengths the employee is bringing to the organization and the role, what aspects of the role the employee derives his/her energy from and what feels tedious to him/her, and where the employee feels he/she needs to leverage additional time in the training for comfortability.

- Alignment between the employee and manager, on the expectation for the employee to bring his/her job description to life. Similarly, there should be a mutual understanding of roles and responsibilities both independent and collaborative.

- Key partnerships that will require collaboration should be discussed as part of the training. The employee should also be given opportunities to build relationships with some of these key partners during the training process. This will allow the collaboration post training to be executed with more comfortability and confidence. It can also allow for a feeling of personal connection to others on the team before formally working with them.

- The learning styles we previously discussed should be considered to determine how to immerse the employee in the training whether that be through a majority of hands on training, classroom style training, web-based training, etc.

- There should be a pre-identified routine for check-in. It's critical that the manager communicates in advance when and how he/she will check in to ensure the training is effective and that the employee feels he/she has the needed support desired. The more frequent the check-in, the easier it is to re-direct or to make revisions to the training in the moment.

Meaningful Mentorship

Mentorship provides VIP access to the experience, skill and knowledge of proven leaders that you wouldn't otherwise be privy to. It allows for a mutual relationship that benefits both individuals and adds value to the company. In my leadership journey my development has been most influenced by mentorship. And, I would say that the impact has been from being on both sides of the table. Being a mentee inspired me to be a mentor to others.

The hardest part about being a mentee can be getting the buy-in and commitment of a key leader to make you and your development a priority. I've found that taking the initiative to build a relationship with the desired mentor by initially focusing on what is important to him/her will get his/her attention. Once you have their attention and the foundation of a relationship; you can start to share your story, your leadership, your goals.

Mentorship should provide support and empowerment for the mentee inclusive of some or all of the key advantages it has to offer.

- Encouragement and increased confidence
- Progress towards career goals
- Improved leadership competencies
- Growth in professional maturity
- A learning environment that teaches new skills
- Diversity of perspective
- Enhanced personal brand
- Increased visibility and network
- Better communication skills

As a mentor you will need to be purposeful about your partnership with the mentee to ensure that several of these materialize as key benefits from their point of view.

- Have a questions-based dialogue with your mentee to understand his/her personality, how he/she communicates, the state of his/her leadership, how he/she believes your partnership will be best utilized.

- Give the mentee an invitation to get to know you as a person. Your title alone may be intimidating to your mentee. Allowing him/her to get to know you beyond the title will make the mentee feel more comfortable trusting and interacting with you.

- Ask your mentee for 1-2 goals he/she would like to focus on. Create a development plan with behavioral steps or activities that would help he/she achieve those goals. Make sure the mentee has bought in to the plan as effective.

- Plan each session at least a day prior to when it is scheduled, so that it is clear you are prepared and making it a priority.

- Provide direct feedback balanced with suggestions and encouragement as needed in each session to eliminate gray area for the mentee and to continue to build trust.

- Ask your mentee for feedback around how he/she feels you are supporting him/her and make adjustment within reason.

- Create shared moments for celebrating success. Give recognition and have a genuine pride in the mentee's developmental progress.

Coaching the Coach

Many can coach those that make up the employee base. Only the elite few do a truly exceptional job of leading and coaching other leaders to be exceptional as well. When you have the responsibility of "coaching the coach" or coaching those that lead others, that responsibility includes helping leaders work more purposefully and to help identify areas of leadership where they can be more effective and/or efficient. Just like an athletic coach, a leader as a coach can improve how he/she helps another leader fully leverage strengths by making it a habit of "studying the tapes." In the case of leadership, it is observing and studying live tapes of your leader's behavior to understand habits in his/her behavior and to be more effective in revealing blind spots and giving feedback.

The coach to coach relationship must be collaborative and individualized working towards an agreed upon destination via leader-to-leader partnership. The relationship must be made up of tailored developmental interactions. The senior coach must function as a resource and champion. To be a resource that is as value added as possible, there are several things that a manager can do to effectively coach the coach and help the leader knock his/her personal leadership out of the park.

- ➢ Help the leader identify ways to continue to raise the bar.
- ➢ Grow the leader's mindset with challenging, self-reflective questions.
- ➢ Conduct and provide a 360 degree assessment and feedback from the leader's peers and team.

Differentiated Leadership

- Teach the leader how to develop and engage in succession planning routines.

- Provide real life examples of how to manage "different or controversial" leaders on their team and how to coach them.

- Practice interactions with the leader to help them improve their ability to have crucial conversations or tough talks.

- Role play with the leader to give them confidence in their ability to manage up.

- Teach them how to challenge the status quo.

- Help the leader to keep up with an increasingly fast-moving professional environment.

- Show the leader how to narrowly define vision and ensure that all of their efforts and direction are connected to it.

- Empower the leader to evolve their growth mindset.

- Give the leader examples of how to remove emotions from situations as necessary.

- Teach them how to focus on the future while engaging in the moment, the balance of consistent execution and vision coupled with strategy.

- Put the leader in situations that allow him/her to practice and increase command presence.

- ➢ Help the leader create a personalized environment of learning for sustainment of growth and progress.

- ➢ Be transparent about the leader's points of resistance to enhance personal awareness.

- ➢ Walk through ways to play on the strengths of the team.

- ➢ Teach them how to consistently and tactically follow up on the follow up.

- ➢ Provide insight on his/her strategy development, implementation and execution through the team.

As parents our job is to create an environment and lead our children to be as successful as possible. We have to draw on our own experiences, tap into our creative intelligence and seek partnership or advice when applicable to enhance our decision making. Tough conversations are part of the parental role. Without them our children would be unclear about what is acceptable and what isn't, to what degree they can test the boundaries, and they will be less likely to meet their full potential.

While I wouldn't co-sign on taking on a parental role in the professional environment, I do see inferences relative to leadership. As leaders we are paid, and hopefully self-inspired, to lead others to be as successful as their potential and capability will allow. We influence based on the sum of experiences and learnings we have had in our leadership journey. We use our education and intellectual horsepower. We partner with others who have had similar experiences or have helpful expertise to make effective decisions.

Most leaders also desire the ability to be more confident when they have to give constructive feedback or have a crucial conversation. After all, it is our responsibility to hold leaders accountable when they stray from committed expectations no matter how uncomfortable the conversations feel to us. It is our job to have the uncomfortable conversation that may make a leader uncomfortable in the short term. The purpose is so that the leader can be comfortable, confident and improvingly successful in the long term. That purpose is only realized if we have the conversation in an effective manner with confidence.

Complete confidence in having tough conversations will take practice. The good news is, there are several things we can do to improve and make each tough conversation more effective than the last.

1. Prepare in advance.
    a. The best preparation starts long before you need to have a tough conversation. Any prior conversations informal or formal around his/her leadership or performance should be documented. Get in the habit of taking notes. Use the

notes to build on the conversation each time. When you have a tough conversation, it shouldn't be a surprise.
  b. Gather any relevant facts to minimize the emotion of the dialogue and to keep the conversation on track. These facts may include financials, customer or client feedback, employee feedback, notes from previous conversations, job description, an email that provided company direction, etc.
  c. Also prepare for how the leader may react. Is he/she an emotional leader, does he/she tend to respond with excuses, is he/she aggressive and defensive in his/her reactions? Your preparation should include how you will respond to keep the conversation professional and aligned on the topic at hand.

2. Have the conversation as soon as feasibly possible. Your urgency will let the leader know that it's serious and important.

3. Approach the conversation in a questions-based manner.
    a. Start off by asking the leader his/her thoughts on why you called the meeting. Reinforce accurate assessment and clarify where he/she may not be on the same page.
    b. Ask the leader if he/she understands the importance of what has been asked.
    c. Ask him/her if expectations will be executed as a commitment. If so, be genuine in communicating that you are there as a support partner and let him/her define what support looks like. If not, let

> the leader know what the options are for the way forward.

4. If the leader gets side tracked in conversation or starts to point fingers stop the communication and remind him/her of the focus of the conversation. Re-direct them back to the needed dialogue.

5. Make sure respect remains mutual on both sides. Be professional with the leader and show that you respect the positive aspects of his/her leadership. Don't allow the leader to raise his/her voice, swear at you or respond in any way that is disrespectful.

6. End the conversation in a way that the leader knows there is a separation between personal and business.

7. Re-instill confidence in the leader, shake his/her hand, smile.

The more painful the conversation seems, the more indicative that the conversation is crucial and needs to take priority. The tougher it feels, the more the senior leader will need to lean into the interaction. The more the senior leader needs to lean in, the more he/she must lead in an effort to benefit his/her leader and impact his/her leader's growth.

Conflict management is one of the least 'sexy' responsibilities of leadership but one of the most critical. Leadership is a contact sport, and because of that, conflict in the workplace will always exist and will require direct and consistent involvement. Types of conflict may include disagreements, power struggles, public lack of respect for position or authority, blatant breach of trust, harassment.

Allowing for a degree of conflict can stimulate strategy and/or innovation. However, if a leader does not shut down the behaviors causing the conflict, it can fuel an unhealthy environment.

An environment where conflict has become part of the culture will show symptoms of visible anger in tone, facial expressions, communication, arguments, complaining, withdrawing, one person refusing to work with the other person, etc. These symptoms have big impact and the ripple effects can be:

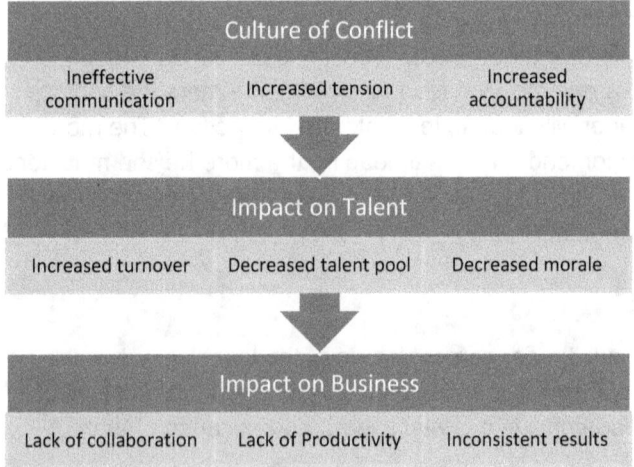

Differentiated Leadership

Because each of these are such a big impact on an organization, ignoring conflict or procrastinating relative to conflict can cause a positive work environment and culture to deteriorate. It can cause a team or business to fail. It is also a sign of ineffective leadership.

In the best-case scenario, conflict can be an opportunity for learning and growth. To make that opportunity a reality there are several things leaders must consider and/or do.

- ➤ Before engaging in the resolution discussion, decide what you will do as the leader if conflict goes unresolved.

- ➤ Identify and speak with any witnesses that may be able to provide perspective on the situation.

- ➤ Sit down with each person individually and then together to keep an aligned focus when the conversation becomes a group activity.

- ➤ Provide a meeting setting that is considered neutral territory. Avoid using someone's office.

- ➤ Function as the mediator if you are the manager.

- ➤ Give those involved the opportunity to calm down and work through initial emotions.

- ➤ Encourage each person to adopt a mindset where he/she assumes positive intent.

- Remind everyone to focus the dialogue on facts and behavior versus on personalizing it with emotion.

- Re-direct the conversation any time the dialogue becomes fueled by emotion.

- Clearly communicate both areas of agreement and disagreement.

- Prioritize the areas of conflict.

- Solicit and share things each person can do to manage the conflict in a productive manner going forward.

- Require each person to actively listen. Have each person repeat what he/she took away from what the other person said.

- Have each person share how they like to be communicated to and interacted with in the work environment.

- Have each person self-reflect and communicate his/her role in the conflict.

- Communicate that there will be accountability for not resolving differences as it will be the responsibility of those in conflict to find a way to reflect professionalism.

- Determine follow-up/check-in points.

- Provide any necessary training.

- Lead by example.

> Collaborate with Human Resources so that they are in the loop and prepared to be an active partner if needed.

Often a taboo aspect of business, performance management tends to be the caution sign at an employee's fork in the road. When an employee reaches this point, he/she has two choices. The choice to focus and get execution and results back on track with urgency, or the choice to be performance managed out of the business will be behaviorally dictated. It is not enough for an employee to verbally communicate that they want to improve performance. Behavioral communication and its ability to be evidenced in results will be the deciding factor.

Part of the success of the performance management process falls on the manager of the employee. An actionable plan should be written, communicated and followed up on weekly to provide the employee the opportunity to end up on the positive side of the metaphorical fork in the road. The perception the senior leader gives to the employee about his/her continued confidence and investment in him/her to turn the performance around has a lot of influence.

10

BUILDING A COHESIVE AND EFFECTIVE TEAM

Team cohesion is the degree to which each member of the team is willing and able to work together to be effective and bring the company vision and mission to life. It is the evident way a team interacts with each other to ensure goals are achieved. It is all members of the team being aligned around what's most important and the commitment to keep those things priority.

An effective team starts with relationships. First, the leader must build a relationship with each individual employee or leader on the team. The leader should make consistent efforts to understand who each employee is outside of work and how that translates to who each employee is in the work environment. The leader should seek to understand each employee's personality, hobbies, family, whether he/she is an introvert or extrovert, what talents he/she possesses. The leader should also be willing to be transparent, so the connection is mutual. A leader can share things that are not work related without dismissing personal privacy.

Once a personal connection is made there should be a focus on the professional connection. The leader should ask probing questions to gain insight about the employee's strengths and the things that are challenges. The leader should find out what drives or motivates him/her and what activities feel draining. He/she should find out the employee's learning style as well as how each employee likes to be led. There should be an assessment of the employee's aptitude and capacity to understand and execute different levels of thinking and processes.

After building a relationship between the leader and each employee on the team, the leader should spend time connecting to the team as a whole. Meetings, conference calls, team buildings can be a great backdrop for the leader to connect with the collective team. Members of the collective team should also have peer-to-peer relationships. The leader could require and find ways to enable teamwork and collaboration. There could be an implementation of peer-to-peer recognition built into the weekly or monthly routines. For example, to start off each conference call team members could be required to provide recognition to one of their peers. There could also be peer-to-peer training and coaching.

Assuming all relationships have been established, there are some tactics that have proved beneficial in enabling effective teams.

- ➢ Make sure it is a diverse team of thought, gender, experience, ability and ethnicity.
- ➢ Provide team bumpers-guidelines by which each team member must abide.
- ➢ Create peer partnerships or buddies. Be sure that each one has a different strength so they have something to contribute to one another.
- ➢ Have regular meetings/conference calls to increase interaction of the team.
- ➢ Provide cross-functional training.
- ➢ Involve different members of the team in the selection of additional talent.
- ➢ Volunteer in the community as a team.
- ➢ Create a culture of team learning.
- ➢ Celebrate collaborative successes.
- ➢ Promote vulnerability in conversation amongst the team.
- ➢ Help resolve conflicts quickly and professionally.
- ➢ Don't take yourself or let the members of the team take themselves too seriously.

While the investment in building and growing a team to its maximum potential of effectiveness may seem too tedious a task, the effort is well worth the return. Effective teams have better morale leading to better engagement. They have team members with a higher than average level of confidence. They have team members that are more loyal to the team, their leader and the company which has a positive impact on retention. And, teams that are cohesive and effective attract top talent much more easily than others. In sum, these benefits have been proven to help a company achieve incremental financial gains long term.

11

DECISION MAKING THAT MAKE SENSE

According to John C. Maxwell, inability to make decisions is one of the principal reasons executives fail. Deficiency in decision making ranks much higher than lack of specific knowledge or technical know-how as an indicator of leadership failure. Things to consider to ensure effective decision making:

> *Timing*-Even in moments of uncertainty or lack of clarity the timing or timeliness of a decision can deem it effective or ineffective. A decision can be made pre-maturely or a decision can be made at the point where it has become irrelevant.

    o Premature decision making occurs when a leader is simply being impulsive with no thought put into the decision, assumptive without merit of reason, or with underestimation of the true impact a decision can have on other things.

- o Late decision making is common with leaders who tend to procrastinate. In some cases, taking too long may cause a situation to be the unintended decision maker. For instance, if a leader suspends an employee and is taking too long deciding whether or not to terminate the employee, that employee may very well quit based on the assumption or fear that he/she will lose his/her job because there wasn't any follow up communication. If the leader decided he wanted to retain the employee, that leader has now caused unnecessary turnover. If the leader made the decision to terminate the employee, the leader then loses the ability to code the termination as involuntary and non-re-hirable because the employee opted out prior to official termination.

➢ *Justification* is a leader's way of showing or giving reason to why a particular decision was made. If the leader has no valid or convicted rationale for why a particular decision was made, it may be seen as ineffective.

➢ *Precedent* is often a necessary consideration in decision making particularly when it is a higher risk decision or may have people or financial impacts. In a situation that could result in legal ramifications, taking the time to research and understand what decision has been made in a similar situation improves the effectiveness of the decision.

> *Impact* should be taken into account in effective decision making as it implicates what or who will be affected by the decision, and to what degree they will be affected.

> *Input* or consideration of other points of view, experience and expertise can improve the quality of a decision, because it allows the subject of the decision to be looked at from the lens of various thought processes. This allows the primary decision maker to take additional things into account that may not have been considered.

In addition to the consideration of the things that can help to improve decision making, some leaders need support or development to be consistently effective. The following are ways that can provide personal growth in the area of decision making.

- Continuing Education
- Mentoring
- Stretch Assignments
- Shadowing of a leader with a strength in decision making
- Practice in partnership with another leader including role plays or example scenarios
- Cross functional training and/or partnership

When making decisions the **T.H.I.N.K. model** is a quick reminder to help you be more effective in the moment.

> **T-Timing**
>   o Take the time to consider relevant info and points of view without procrastinating

to the point of the decision becoming irrelevant or ineffective.

➤ H-Heightened Awareness
- Have a heightened awareness of potential consequences and the impacts of the decision on others and to the company.

➤ I-Identify
- Identify resources that would be important for collaboration.
- Identify a contingency plan. If for some reason a decision doesn't work out based on it being ineffective, based on the situation changing or based on the surfacing of additional relevant information, have a back-up plan in advance.

➤ N-Navigate
- Navigate through the varying points of view and direct the course of the ultimate decision.

➤ K-Keep in Mind
- Keep in mind the end or long-term goal. Make sure the decision keeps the company headed in the direction as outlined in the overall strategy and guided by the vision.

12

GOAL SETTING AND STRATEGY

According to a Harvard Study, those who create a plan, execute the plan, and assess where they are to their goals throughout phases of execution perform 30% better than leaders that don't. Goal setting provides the answer to the five W's in the context of leadership. It determines *what* the leader wants to accomplish, *when* tactics to achieve the goals need to occur, *why* the actions or behaviors are relevant or important, *who* will be executing the behaviors, and *where* the leader is headed versus where the leader is today. Goal setting is about creating the bar of expectation and giving clear guidance on how to execute at that level.

For goal setting to be successful it must involve key aspects in the process.

- The goals must be specific and tied to behaviors for execution.

- An action plan for execution should be broken down into achievable steps.

- Clear communication to the necessary people about what the goals are and what their expected role is in meeting those goals has to be a priority.

- The goal must be able to be tangibly measured through key performance indicators, financials, customer loyalty metrics, etc.

- Accountability around tracking towards the goals and achieving the goals by the target date must exist.

It is important to remember that the goals should challenge people to continue to improve productivity, experience or financial results. However, it is equally as important that the goal setting process does not create a bar of expectation so low that people can step over it. Goals that are too easily achieved do not improve a company's success or the growth of its leaders. This type of ineffective goal setting can create a culture of mediocrity.

Leaders at any level are accountable for execution. Execution in lieu of planning is risky at best. Planning is the leader's blueprint or map for execution. Without it a company could be aimlessly headed in the wrong direction, a team may not have an aligned focus, and objectives will likely not be clear. According to Dun and

Bradstreet, 50% of new businesses fail within the first two years and 75% within the first 3 years commonly due to the lack of or ineffective planning. Planning must be prioritized and purposeful as it is the launchpad for execution.

Purposeful or strategic planning is the process of creating a leadership map or navigational system that gives the company guidance on the direction to take. The leader is the one who has primary responsibility for building the plan and functioning as the "GPS" in cases where a team is off course and needs to be re-routed or re-directed. Essentially, the leader is the link between the creation of the plan and the execution of the plan.

13

ADOPTING AN ENTREPRENEURIAL MINDSET

Success in any professional environment depends strongly on the ability of a leader to develop new, innovative, and strategic ideas. Leaders with an entrepreneurial mindset are committed to and inspired by the opportunity to create their own success. They are determined not to let anyone else dictate their personal or professional journey. They have the ability to see the future and the potential future. The entrepreneurial mindset is a state of mind that possesses a strong desire to understand who potential clients are, what needs they have, and then are compelled to be the one who meets those needs most effectively. It is a state of mind that thrives on setting up camp outside their comfort zone.

Leaders with an entrepreneurial mindset have the ability to see opportunity that is not visible or does not feel achievable to others. They execute based on the presence of opportunity versus executing based off of direction given by others. They always do more than expected and see the requirement or goal as a minimum expectation. They have a healthy and above average level of self-accountability and are always questioning the why behind what they are doing and how it contributes to the company's purpose.

The mindset of an entrepreneur brings the leader to life as a networking guru. The entrepreneurial leader seeks out relevant connections and forms collaboration with those connections to help accelerate the growth of the business. He/she sources and surrounds himself/herself with talent from a non-traditional talent pool. Once a team is formed, the entrepreneurial leader becomes strategic in how he/she delegates to those team members to get the most from the least amount of needed people. A leader with an entrepreneurial mindset becomes a master of implementation and doesn't allow those on the team to have a "wait and see" point of view. The leader and the team ensure that every day is planned in such a way that it moves the company closer to the ultimate goal.

The entrepreneurial mindset gives a leader a "fake it 'til you make it" mentality. He/she gains the ability to portray confidence in doing things he/she has never done before but are necessary to move the business forward. They

Differentiated Leadership

learn through trial and error, they find momentum even while leading through areas of gray. While most leaders have a fear of failure, these leaders accept and utilize failure as part of the process of maximizing the company's potential and performance.

Make it a point to grow your entrepreneurial mindset:

- Connect your plans and action steps back to your company's vision daily or at least weekly.

- Invest in your learning, read books relative to entrepreneurship.

- Be disciplined in alignment of the company's vision and long-term goals but be a leader that takes risks on the company's behalf. Take action with an innovative thought process and with urgency.

- Look for innovative ways to improve your company's current processes and strategies and share those ideas with key decision makers.

- Focus more on how you can continually evolve the experiences that give the company mobility than on the actual outcomes.

- Constantly take the initiative to strengthen and broaden your network.

- Look below the surface of situations. Find and point out the silver linings and opportunities that come from challenges versus focusing on the negative.

- Position yourself to be as open about your imperfections as you are about your accomplishments. Accept failure and learnings as part of the process of growing an entrepreneurial mindset.

IN CONCLUSION

I challenge you not to want to be different, not to desire to be different, not to just say you want to be different but to dare to truly represent the epitome of differentiated leadership. Find the courage to be different when it is necessary. Find the voice to be different when it matters. Find the ability to always be present without having to be visible. Find a way to step outside your comfort zone and become an expert at helping other leaders redefine their zone of comfort. Find that inner fire to spark the necessary intuition and drive that differentiates you from other leaders.

You have to make the decision to differentiate yourself. Hopefully, you find this book useful as a leadership tool. Stick to the blueprint. Understand how leadership can be evident in all aspects of life; master the phases of leadership; work on self-development first.

Make the effort to identify the uniqueness of each leader; become proficient in the skills of leadership; create a limitless learning environment for yourself and others. In moments of doubt or failure, slow down to speed up. Pick up the blueprint and understand your state of leadership in that moment, and allow the tool to meet you where you are. Then, get back to finding ways to meet other leaders where they are, and escort them to their full potential.

ABOUT THE AUTHOR

Kiesha King-Brown is a Certified Executive Coach and Business Consultant with WAZA Enterprises, LLC. She is a talented, creative and strategic leader with more than 18 years of experience growing leaders personally and professionally, teaching leaders how to build strategy to drive business and inspiring leaders to exceed expectations.

Kiesha has spent the majority of her career as a Business Executive complimented by several years as an HR Executive. She is a subject matter expert in assessing leaders as individuals and connecting with them as people. She connects through her calm and confident, humble and humorous, strategic and savvy personality.

Connect with KK Brown at www.coachkkb.com

www.ingramcontent.com/pod-product-compliance
Lightning Source LLC
Chambersburg PA
CBHW071408220526
45469CB00004B/1213